GW00993569

NATURAL DISASTERS

Janeen Brian

Contents

Introduction

The Earth is always changing.

Natural disasters are changes which are so great they may cause damage to the shape of the land or cause damage to the lives of people and other living things.

Great changes happen deep inside the Earth and on its surface. The changes on the outer part of the Earth happen because of different kinds of weather.

This book explains seven types of natural disaster. It tells you about their causes and their effects.

Volcanic eruption

A volcanic eruption is the spurting out of gases and hot lava from an opening in the Earth's crust.

Pressure from deep inside the Earth forces ash, gas and molten rock to the surface.

Lava and thick ash can burn or bury towns. When a volcano erupts it may set off an avalanche or a flood.

Fascinating fact
Krakatoa, a volcano in Indonesia, erupted in 1883. The noise of the blast was so loud that it was heard in Australia, 4,828 km (2,998 miles) away.

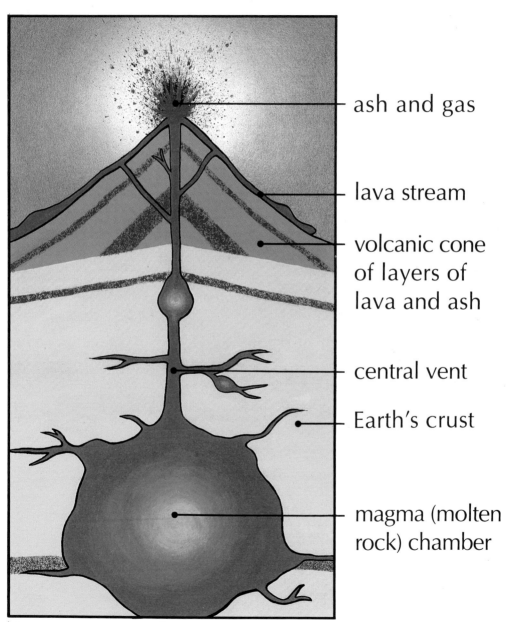

ash and gas

lava stream

volcanic cone
of layers of
lava and ash

central vent

Earth's crust

magma (molten
rock) chamber

Cross-section of a volcano

5

Earthquake

An earthquake is a violent shaking of the ground. Sometimes it is so strong that the ground splits apart.

When plates of rock in the Earth's crust move against one another, giant shock waves move upwards to the surface and cause earthquakes.

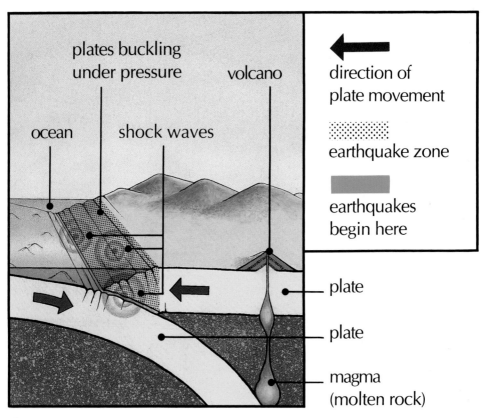

plates buckling under pressure

volcano

direction of plate movement

ocean

shock waves

earthquake zone

earthquakes begin here

plate

plate

magma (molten rock)

Bridge in San Francisco destroyed by earthquake in 1990.

Large earthquakes can:
- rip open roads and fields;
- topple houses and buildings;
- buckle railway tracks;
- cause avalanches and tsunamis (see 'Flood');
- cause death.

Fascinating fact
Some scientists say that cockroaches can sense an earthquake before it happens. The insects rush about in a strange way just before the disaster.

7

Cyclone

A cyclone is a fierce storm with strong winds that spin around in a giant circle. It is also called a *hurricane* or *typhoon* in some parts of the world.

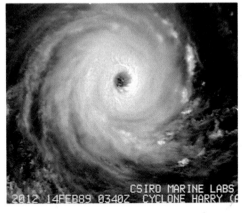

Satellite photo of a cyclone

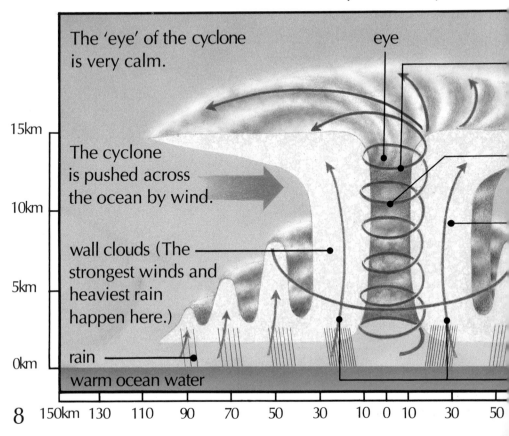

The 'eye' of the cyclone is very calm.

eye

The cyclone is pushed across the ocean by wind.

wall clouds (The strongest winds and heaviest rain happen here.)

rain

warm ocean water

15km

10km

5km

0km

150km 130   110   90   70   50   30   10 0 10   30   50

During a cyclone:
- trees can be uprooted and stripped of leaves;
- buildings can be destroyed;
- cars can be overturned.

4. The giant whirlwind spirals upwards around the 'eye'.

3. The rotation of the Earth makes these clouds spin into a giant whirlwind.

2. As the air rises, it cools, forming rain clouds.

1. Cyclones usually begin near the equator where warm, wet air rises from the ocean.

Fascinating fact
The winds from a cyclone are so strong they can strip paint off houses, tear clothes off people's backs and twist people's mouths so that they cannot speak.

Cross-section of a cyclone

90   110   130   150km   land

9

Avalanche

An avalanche is a movement of snow, ice and rock down a mountainside. Avalanches happen suddenly and swiftly, and can move as fast as a racing car (up to 200 km/h; 124 mph).

An avalanche can be set off by:
- a lot of snow melting in a short time;
- snow freezing, melting and freezing again;
- a skier moving across the snow;
- vibrations from a loud noise, or the tremor from an earthquake.

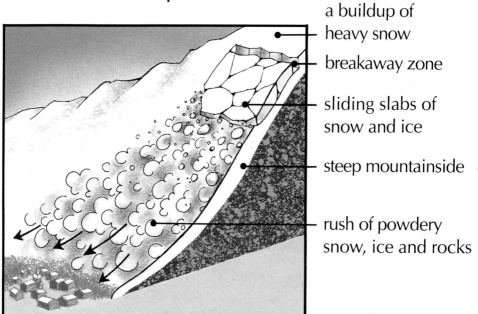

a buildup of heavy snow

breakaway zone

sliding slabs of snow and ice

steep mountainside

rush of powdery snow, ice and rocks

Avalanches can:
- destroy buildings;
- derail trains;
- bury towns and people.

Fascinating fact

An avalanche once caused a tow-truck to be flung from a hotel car park into the second storey of the hotel.

11

Flood

A flood is an overflow of water which covers land that is usually dry. There are two kinds of flood; inland and coastal.

Most inland floods happen when there has been heavy rain or when a lot of snow melts. The water swells rivers and creeks and makes them overflow their banks.

This flood was caused by a river which burst its banks after heavy rain.

Coastal floods are caused by high tides, a rise in sea-level, storm waves and on-shore winds.

Giant waves have swept boats onto the shore. Cars and buildings were damaged in this coastal flood caused by a tsunami.

Fascinating fact

Giant waves, called *tsunamis*, are caused by earthquakes beneath the ocean. When the waves reach the shore, they crash suddenly and cause great damage. The tallest recorded tsunami was as tall as a twenty-five storey building.

Drought

A drought is the lack of rain for a long time.

The Sun's heat causes ocean water to evaporate. The water vapour forms clouds and the water returns to Earth as rain. Most parts of the world have a rainy season. A drought may begin if less rain than usual falls during the rainy season.

Lack of rain means crops and grasses die.

Grazing animals may die during a drought through lack of food and water.

Fascinating fact

In 1968 a drought began in Sahel, Africa. Children born during this year were five years old before rain fell again.

Bushfire/Forest fire

A bushfire or forest fire is a fire that burns in bush-
land, grassland or forest.

Fires are caused by lightning, sparks of electricity
or by careless people.

Wind may blow a bushfire to areas where people live.

Fascinating fact
Smoke is the main killer in fires. People and animals
suffocate because they are unable to breathe in oxygen
from the air.

In the Heat of the Moment

Poems by Pauline Prior-Pitt

Drawings by Nancy Upshall

For Robert